Prayer Cor
© 2013 Pa

MW00627863

Paula White Ministries
P. O. Box 58521
Orlando, FL 32858

www.paulawhite.org

Print by: tampaprinter.com

First Edition, 2013
Second Edition, 2015

ISBN #978-0-9861339-0-9

Printed in the United States of America

Abuse

Father, you have rescued me from the dominion of darkness and have brought me into the Kingdom of Light through your Son and love for me. Once I was in darkness, but now I am in your light; I walk as a child of light and not a victim.

I declare all abuse and any symptoms of abuse in my life to be exposed and rebuked by the light of your word and Spirit!

Any history or generational curse of abusive behavior in my family that has caused me to be hostile, angry, filled with rage, depressed and/or abusive is overturned and broken by the supreme power of the blood of Jesus!

I thank you Lord that the evil power of abuse is broken, overthrown and cast down in the name of Jesus. I submit myself to you and resist the devil. I will not have the mindset of a victim. I will not hurt others out of the hurt that has happened to me. I am made whole and restored in the broken places of my soul, heart, body and mind, in the name of Jesus.

I am no longer a victim but an over-comer through Christ Jesus. For Romans 8:37 declares, "No, in all these things we are more than conquerors through Him who loved us."

The abuse I suffered pronounced me guilty and condemned. I was bound and could not lift myself up. You have called me by my name and not my shame. In the name of Jesus I break out of every p rison of abuse; emotional and physical, that has crippled me!

The anointing that is upon you is here to heal the brokenness and wounds of the past. I receive it now in the name of Jesus.

Every power that wants to destroy my live, I command to be destroyed in the name of Jesus!

In Jesus' name I seal off every evil doorway of uncontrollable thoughts in my life from abuse and wounding, by the blood of Jesus.

Notes

_____

_____

_____

_____

_____

_____

_____

_____

_____

_____

_____

_____

_____

_____

_____

_____

_____

_____

_____

_____

_____

_____

Addictions

I thank you, Father, that I am redeemed by the blood of Jesus from the hands of Satan. I am justified and made righteous by the blood of Jesus and belong to you; spirit, soul and body. I renounce any and all addictions that seek to control my life and declare myself free in the name of Jesus!

Father, I confess to you, that in the past through ignorance, curiosity, or willfulness, I have opened doors and come into contact with certain transgressions. I now recognize that as sin and confess it as sin, claiming forgiveness in the name of Jesus. On the basis of the blood of Jesus, I seek complete freedom and deliverance from all addictions in my life. I am free in the name of Jesus and by your grace and blood working on my behalf; I shut every door that would pull me back into bondage!

I ask you, Father, to send your angels to break, cut and sever all fetters, bands, chains and ties of whatever sort the enemy has managed to place on my mind or body by word or by deed. I am free from any and all addictions in Jesus' name!

In the name of Jesus I repent of, renounce and revoke all addictive behaviors in my life!

I claim freedom from addictions because of all the provisions made in 1 John 1:9, which declares the curses broken off of myself and my descendants, in the name of Jesus!

Notes

Adversity

In the name of Jesus I resist and bind every spirit of oppression and heaviness!

Lord, teach me to use every adverse situation and circumstance in my life to bring forth the fruit of Holiness rather than the fruit of sin and wickedness.

Lord, you promised me in Isaiah 54:17 that no weapon formed against me would be able to prosper and that every tongue that rises against me would be condemned. In the name of Jesus I declare that the weapons of mass destruction the enemy would use against me are destroyed!

Let every door of adversity and attack against my spiritual progress be closed in the name of Jesus!

What the enemy has meant for my destruction, you, Lord have already turned around to work for the good for your purpose and plan in my life in Jesus' name! (Romans 8:28)

Notes

Affiliations

Father, give me heightened discernment, particularly with those I designate as friends and associates. May your divine purpose simplify my life. I refuse and reject the embrace of magnetizers of destruction, in the name of Jesus!

In the name of Jesus I call into my life the spiritual connections that strategically align me with the will of God for my purpose, assignment, calling and destiny!

In the name of Jesus I declare this to be a time of divine favor and uninhibited access to people and places that are connected to the fullness of the will of God for my life!

Lord, you know all things. Man looks on the outside and you see from the heart and inside of a person. Reveal to me every demonic set up, trap and snare that the enemy has for me through those that are closest to me. Give me the wisdom and the courage to let go of every detrimental relationship and association, in the name of Jesus.

Father I ask you to send laborers to reap the harvest of souls and strengthen me to fulfill the assignment in the field you have planted me in and let it be for your glory.

In the name of Jesus I pray that I walk in the image and likeness of you, God, to be a living testimony of your goodness, grace and glory to all those that I come in contact with.

7

Anger

Lord I ask that you free me from the root of every problem, curse and cause that creates anger in me. I bring my spirit, flesh and mind under the control and influence of the Holy Spirit. You have given me the fruit of patience and long suffering. I ask that you fully develop your character and the fruits of the spirit in my life.

Lord I command every area of my life in which the devil is holding me captive by a spirit of anger, rage or wrath, to be loosed in the name of Jesus!

In the name of Jesus I forgive and release every person who has wronged me knowingly or unknowingly that has caused a door to be opened for anger and resentment to enter in!

I command every spirit of anger to go and the spirit of freedom to come to me by the blood of Jesus! In the name of Jesus I will not lose self-control but will be tempered by your precious spirit, Lord, to walk in love, peace and goodness, for your glory.

In the name of Jesus I ask you, Lord, to forgive me for every fit of anger I have allowed to overtake me.

In the name of Jesus I command all the works of the flesh be dismantled in my life!

Lord help to repair all the good altars that anger has broken down in my life.

Lord, help me to control my anger or loss of temper and replace it with forgiveness and compassion.

Please develop and manifest the fruit of your spirit in my life.

Notes

_____

_____

_____

_____

_____

_____

_____

_____

_____

_____

_____

_____

_____

_____

_____

_____

_____

_____

_____

_____

_____

_____

_____

_____

_____

_____

_____

_____

_____

Anointing

Today I confess my sins and repent to you God for anything known or unknown that would separate me from intimacy with you and your anointing manifesting in my life.

In Christ Jesus, I receive the anointing that teaches me all things.

I am in agreement with your word in Luke 4:18-19 which states, "The Spirit of the Lord is on me, because He has anointed me to preach the good news to the poor. He has sent me to proclaim freedom for the prisoners and recovery of sight for the blind, to release the oppressed, to proclaim the year of the Lord's favor."

I decree and declare that I am anointed and empowered to pursue and overtake all forces of wickedness and to recover all stolen items from the enemy!

I ask you, Lord, for an increase of your anointing for every challenge that is ahead of me and to release fresh oil in my life so that I will not be dry, brittle and hardened by hardships, weariness and obstacles that I may face.

In the name of Jesus I receive the anointing of God for every weak moment in my life.

I decree and declare there is an anointing of ease on my life, my family, my relationships, my ministry and my purpose! I deploy the hand of God to work for me at all times, in Jesus' name.

Lord, anoint me to bring glory to you in every area of my life. Give me power to resist the devil so that he will flee from me.

Notes

_____

_____

_____

_____

_____

_____

_____

_____

_____

_____

_____

_____

_____

_____

_____

_____

_____

_____

_____

_____

_____

_____

_____

_____

_____

_____

_____

_____

_____

_____

_____

Attitude

According to your word Lord, I have the mind of
Christ to hold the thoughts and feelings of the
Messiah. I determine my attitude to be one of
gratitude and hope. Allow me to see with your eyes
of understanding, in the name of Jesus.

Lord, by your Holy Spirit, perfect the fruit of my lips.
Help me give thanks from my inner-most being.
Reach down into the most secret places of my heart
that I may offer thanksgiving to you, Father. I will
bless and love others by the grace you have given me
in the name of Jesus.

With my soul I will bless the Lord with every
thought and purpose in my life. My heart, mind and
attitude will be pleasing to you, Lord, and shall not
wander out of your presence. My life will glorify the
Father; spirit, soul and body. I will not hold grudges
and will take no thought of the evil done to me. I will
pay no attention to any suffered wrongs, and they
shall hold no place in my thought life, attitude and
perspective. I am ready to see every person through
the eyes of Christ, the name by which I pray.

Notes

Balance

Father, you know every area in my life that is out of balance. I ask that you reveal to me by your spirit how to walk with equilibrium and not burn out or be weary in well doing.

I command every sin that would so easily beset me and every weight that would burden me to be removed in the name of Jesus!

Lord you have called me to live a life in the Kingdom that is active, blessed and fruitful. I will not stress out or worry about things that create imbalances in my life. I trust you and give my every day needs over to you. I seek you first and by doing so; know that everything I have need of will be added to my life in the name of Jesus.

Notes

Barrenness

In the name of Jesus I command the curse and addition of barrenness to be broken off of my life and my purpose! I am fruitful, effective and blessed beyond measure as a child of the Most High God!

In the name of Jesus I denounce and renounce any covenant of barrenness formed consciously or unconsciously, whether by me or on my behalf.

Lord let the power of the Holy Spirit overshadow me. Every dry, unproductive, ineffective, barren place will be flooded by your presence and watered by your spirit, in the name of Jesus!

In the name of Jesus I am filled with the goodness of God and produce His blessings in the fruit of my womb, my life, my business, my purpose, my family and all that I set my hand to!

Notes

Belief

Father I thank you for fortifying my belief in you and all that you have for me in your word.

Lord, you said in John 1:12 that as many as received Him to them He gave power to become the sons of God, even to them that believe on His name.

Matthew 18:18 decrees "Verily I say unto you, whatsoever you shall bind on earth shall be bound in heaven: and whatsoever you shall loose on earth shall be loosed in heaven". Therefore in the name of Jesus I bind every spirit of doubt, fear and unbelief that would try to function and operate in my life!

I break every demonic stronghold that seeks to paralyze my belief in the name of Jesus.
Your word declares in John 20:29 "Jesus saith unto him, Thomas, because thou hast seen me, thou hast believed: blessed are they that have not seen, and yet have believed."

Notes

Bitterness

Father I ask in the name of Jesus that you reveal
every root, every seed of bitterness that has been
planted in my life. I repent of, renounce, and reject it
and ask that the blood of Jesus uproot all bitterness.

I forgive every person, situation and event that has
caused wounding, hurt and offense in my life. In the
name of Jesus I refuse to allow bitterness to take
root!

In the name of Jesus I command every pipeline of
bitterness in my life to be consumed by the fire of
God!

You spirit of bitterness, loose your grip over my life,
in the name of Jesus!

Notes

Blessing

The Lord is my shepherd, I shall not want. I fare well, flourish and financially thrive, enjoying success and security to the glory of God so that I may be a blessing to mankind.

In the name of Jesus I command the angels of the living God to roll away the stone blocking my financial, physical and spiritual breakthroughs!

In the name of Jesus I bind every spirit blocking my benefactors from blessing me!

In the name of Jesus let the fire of God melt away the stones hindering my blessings.

Lord, give to me all keys to my goodness that are still in the possession of the enemy.

In the name of Jesus I declare this year to be the year of the beginning of great things in my life, with no limitations, but with the abundant life of Christ freely flowing in every area of my life!

According to your word, let all the blessings prepared and assigned to me be released and come to me from the North, South, East and West.

Lord rain abundant blessings over myself and my family in the name of Jesus! I take possession and live in my land of Canaan.

Notes

Blocking Demonic Assignments

Let every satanic giant standing against me begin to
fall as Goliath under David's hand.

By the blood of Jesus I declare that every arrow that
has been shot at me shall ricochet off and miss its
mark!

In the name of Jesus I remove my name from the
book of the seers of goodness without there being
manifestation.

In the name of Jesus let all secrets of the enemy in
the camp of my life which are still hidden in darkness
be revealed to me!

In the name of Jesus I overturn, arrest, block and
break every snare and trap the enemy has set for me,
my family and my purpose!

The blood of Jesus speaks on my behalf for my
spiritual walk, my emotions, my mind, my health, my
family, my finances and all that concerns my life. In
the name of Jesus no weapon formed against me will
be able to prosper!

I plead the blood of Jesus over the portals of my
mind, my body (the temple of the Holy Spirit), my
emotions and my will.

Notes

Boldness

Father I receive boldness now, in the name of Jesus! Therefore, I have boldness to enter into the Holy of Holies by the blood of Jesus. Because of my faith in you, I dare to have the boldness, courage and confidence of free access (an unreserved approach) to you with freedom and without fear.

In the name of Jesus I break every spirit of timidity and ask the Holy Spirit to release boldness in me so that I may be a witness for the Lord and fulfill His will in my life.

I will be bold toward every demonic and evil spirit, sickness, disease and poverty; for Jesus is the head of all rule and authority. He has disarmed those who were against me. Jesus made a bold display and public example of them by triumphing over them. He has now given me authority by His blood, therefore I am bold to declare that Satan is a defeated foe, in the name of Jesus!

Notes

Bondage

In the name of Jesus I break every captivity that +- has had me bound me since my mother's womb!

Lord I command every area of my life, which the devil is holding in captivity, to be loosed in the name of Jesus! By the revelation of the Holy Spirit make known to me every door of entry into my life by which the enemy has an advantage over me. I shut those doors and entry point by the blood of Jesus!

In the name of Jesus I release myself, my purpose, my family, my finances and my goodness from the hands of evil captivity. I command every spirit that binds and restricts me to go and the spirit of freedom to come, in Jesus name!

I command every fetter and chain that is holding back my spiritual progression to be broken by the blood of Jesus!

Breaking Yokes

I command all stubborn yokes be broken in the name of Jesus!

Lord, your anointing destroys the yoke. Let every yoke on me, my family, my purpose, my finances, my children, my health, my mind and every area of my life be destroyed by your anointing!

In the name of Jesus every yoke from the sins of my forefathers is broken off of me and my lineage. Father I come to you and confess that my forefathers and I have sinned. I repent and ask for the blood of Jesus to redeem me and my household.

Notes

Burdens

Lord God, thank you for your presence! I choose to lift up my eyes and see your goodness, grace and love in my life. I give every burden and weight over to you. By the blood of Jesus I will live free and clear of all hindrances, afflictions and hardships that load me down. I decree and declare that every good gift my heavenly Father has for me is released in the name of Jesus! I have LIFE more abundantly through Jesus Christ! I reject every evil spiritual load placed on me and command it to be removed! I will not carry any weight of anxiety, stress and pressure in my mind, body, soul or spirit.

In Jesus' name I break all bonds and overturn any load the enemy wants to burden me with; un-forgiveness, bitterness, and resentment. I cut off the root of everything that creates burdens in my life and shut the door to all anxiety, by the blood of Jesus!

I command every stubborn yoke (burden) in my life, family and relationships to be broken, in Jesus' name! I declare the peace of God to rule and reign in my heart where there has been stress.

Career

I ask for your wisdom, Lord, to be effective in my labor and to glorify you in everything I do in my workplace. Let the light of Christ shine through me that others who I work with will see and know who you are.

Father I commit my works (the plans and cares of my business) to you. I entrust them to you wholly. Since you effectually work in me, you cause my thoughts to become agreeable with your will, so that my business plans will be established and succeed. I thank you for giving to me by your gracious favor every kind of wisdom, practical insight and prudence and in the name of Jesus I submit myself to them.

Lord I deploy angels, the ministering spirits you have assigned to me, to go forth and bring in resources, contracts, people and everything necessary for my business to prosper and flourish, in the name of Jesus!

In the name of Jesus, Father give me knowledge and skill in the areas where I am inexperienced.

In the name of Jesus I speak success, favor and prosperity over everything that I do in accordance to your will for my business.

I walk in and receive the kingly anointing to prosper and advance the kingdom of God for your glory, Lord.

Children

Lord I recognize and confess that my children are a blessing from you. I make a vow to bring them up in the fear and the caution of you and to teach them your ways. My children will grow to know and love you, Lord. They will walk in the plan and purpose you have designed for them. Give me the wisdom to discern and navigate their gifting, calling and destiny, in the name of Jesus.

I declare that no weapon formed against my children will be able to prosper! My children are protected by the blood of Jesus! When they go to school, work or play, no harm will come to them!

In the name of Jesus I break any covenant made with death, hell and the grave over my children! The enemy will not have them and they shall serve God all the days of their lives!

You promised in your word, Psalm 128:3, that my children will be like olive plants round about my table. Therefore they will be off-shoots of my relationship with you.

Father you promised in your word that you would pour your spirit upon my seed and your blessing upon my offspring. (Isaiah 44:3)

My children are my crown and glory. They will not bring me shame but honor and joy, in the name of Jesus.

Comfort

Though I walk in the midst of trouble, you will revive me: you will stretch forth your hand against the wrath of my enemies, and your right hand will save me. (Psalm 138:7)

I cast all my burdens over to you Lord, knowing that you will sustain me and never allow the righteous to be moved. You are my comforter, Holy Spirit, you keep me in times of trouble and distress.

Lord you are a refuge for the oppressed, a refuge in times of trouble. (Psalm 9:9) I run to you for my comfort and safety. Only your arms have the strength to carry me through life. I completely depend, rely on and trust you as my source for life.

When I am hurting, confused, heavy-laden and burdened; I will come to you Lord for you will give me rest. You are my Sabbath! I find comfort in you and in the name of your Son, Jesus Christ.

Confusion

Today I make a choice to be sober-minded; to be watchful as my adversary the devil prowls around like a roaring lion, seeking someone to devour. (1 Peter 5:8)

Today I command my mind to think on the things that are edifying to my soul.

May the peace of God, which transcends all understanding, guard my heart and mind, in Christ Jesus, according to Philippians 4:7. Help me focus on that which is true, that which is noble, that which is right, that which is pure, that which is lovely, and that which is admirable. If anything is excellent or praiseworthy, help me to think about such things. Whatever I have learned or received or heard from you, help me to put it into practice.

In the name of Jesus today I submit myself to your word, which exposes and judges the very thoughts and purposes of my heart. Your word will bring clarity and order to my life as I submit myself to it.

I bind any spirit that would cause uncertainty and confusion in my mind and render its activity null and void! I come against all fear, depression and doubt, in Jesus' name! For I hold the mind and thoughts of the Messiah!

In the name of Jesus I bind every spirit of confusion and all that would disorient me. I declare I have clarity and freedom in my mind by the blood of Jesus!

41

I command all disorder, strife and division to cease in my life, ministry, relationships and home, in Jesus' name! I decree unity and peace to prevail and I bring myself in alignment with the order God has set in His word! Holy Spirit, help me to submit to divine order so that the enemy does not get an advantage over me or my family.

Notes

_____

_____

_____

_____

_____

_____

_____

_____

_____

_____

_____

_____

_____

_____

_____

_____

_____

_____

_____

_____

_____

_____

_____

_____

_____

Conquer

I am a world overcomer because I am born of God. I represent the Father and Jesus well. I am a useful member in the House of God and the Body of Christ. I am His workmanship created in Christ Jesus. My Father God is all the while effectually at work in me, both to will and to do His good pleasure. I am effective for the Kingdom and glory of God. (1 John 5:4-5, Ephesians 2:10, Philippians 2:13)

I praise you, Lord because the gates of hell shall not prevail against your church or my purpose and assignment.

Thank you, Lord for your promises that are yea and amen. You have made me more than a conqueror through the blood of Jesus Christ!

Thank you, Lord for purchasing victory for me with your blood and giving me power over all things in both heaven and earth.

In the name of Jesus every weapon of wickedness being fashioned against me will not win!

In the name of Jesus I declare that everywhere I go I am blessed of the Lord and highly favored for He has caused me to be an over-comer in all things.

Notes

Courage

I will wait on you Lord and be of good courage and
you will strengthen my heart according to Psalm
27:14.

By the power of Jesus' blood I break every word that
has been spoken over me that was intended to
produce fear and cause dismay! I ask that you give
me courage, Lord, to face and overcome all things by
the blood of Jesus.

According to Psalm 31:24 I will be of good courage
and you will strengthen my heart because I hope in
you, Lord.

Notes

Covenants

Thank you, Lord, for Calvary. Through the shed blood of Jesus I have been given a new covenant based upon better promises. I am grateful that all I need spiritually, emotionally, physically and materially has been provided in the new covenant that Jesus made on my behalf.

Lord, help me to keep my vows and promises. Let me honor all righteous covenants that have been made by me or on my behalf in the name of Jesus.

Let every ungodly covenant be nullified and replaced by righteous covenants according to the power and promise of the cross.

Notes

Curses

In the name of Jesus I renounce and break loose from all evil curses, charms, jinxes, spells, hexes, psychic powers, bewitchments, witchcraft or sorcery which may have been put upon me or my family! I am redeemed by the blood of Jesus!

By the blood of Jesus I release myself from the influence of water spirits, false prophets, any spirits from the animal kingdom or underground world, rules of wickedness and powers of darkness!

In the name of Jesus I renounce and denounce any conscious or unconscious association with familiar spirits!

In the name of Jesus Christ, I now renounce, break and loose myself from all demonic subjection or control and from any ungodly soul-tie! I declare that I am free by the blood of Jesus!

In Jesus' name I break, arrest and overturn any curse that is negatively affecting my spiritual or physical life, which may be in my family, back even ten generations on both sides of my family!

In the name of Jesus I cancel every negative prophesy and word spoken against my life!

Notes

Death

By the superior blood of Jesus, I break any
agreement with death, hell and the grave made over
me, my life, my health and my purpose! I declare a
full long life!

In Jesus' name I renounce and break every form of
death covenant that I have formed or which anyone
has performed on my behalf!

By the blood of Jesus I stand against every covenant
of sudden and premature death!

In the name of Jesus I break every unprofitable
covenant regarding tragedy and untimely death!

Let every plot of the enemy to kill, steal and destroy
me, be revealed and overturned by the blood of
Jesus! I will live and not die! I will be blessed in my
spirit, soul and body with long life in order to live the
abundant life that Christ died to give me.

Notes

Dedication

I dedicate and commit myself fully to you Lord! I am
your child and freely give my life, giftings, talents,
resources and time to you for your use and service. I
yield myself to you completely for the sake of Jesus!

I am bringing supernatural manifestation of the glory
of God into the earth. I am an agent on assignment as
an ambassador of the Most High God! I bring change
and reformation to advance the kingdom of God, for
I am walking in my purpose, created in the image of
God!

In Him I live and move and have my being. I fully
rely on you Lord to equip and preserve me, in the
name of Jesus.

Lord I accept my responsibility in the kingdom of
God and will be a good steward over all that I have
been given and am assigned to do for you.

Lord, give me boldness to be a witness for you. I
rebuke all fear and timidity that would hold me back
from showing and telling others of your goodness.

Holy Spirit, direct me to divine assignments and
supernatural set-ups. I sensitize myself to your voice,
in the name of Jesus!

Notes

Defeating the Strongman

In the name of Jesus reveal the secret of every hidden giant to me!

In the name of Jesus I bind every strongman that is operating against the will of God for my life!

In the name of Jesus I command every mountain of a problem, in every area of my life, to move and be cast into the sea! I will experience the power and victory of the Lord Jesus Christ! He is my strength! Greater is He that is in me than he that is in the world!

Notes

Deliverance

God has delivered me and broken all chains of
bondage by the blood covenant of Jesus Christ! I am
free and walk in complete liberty by the truth of His
word and the power of the Holy Spirit!

Lord, forgive me. I also forgive myself for all my
faults and failures as you have freely forgiven me.

In the name of Jesus Christ, I renounce, break and
loose myself from all demonic subjection or control
and from any ungodly soul-ties that would keep me
bound and subject to my past, to addictions, to flesh,
to emotional instability and to people who are not a
part of my destiny and are not healthy and safe for
me!

In the name of Jesus I break any curse that is
negatively affecting my spiritual or physical life and
the life of my family, even back to ten generations on
both sides!

I confess that my body is the temple of the Holy
Spirit, redeemed, cleansed and sanctified by the
blood of Jesus. Therefore, because of Jesus, Satan
has no more place in and no more power over me!

Let every thought against me be turned to good, in
Jesus' name! I arrest and overturn every word that
has been spoken over me that is contrary to what
your word has to say about me! I am free to walk in
who you have called me to be by the blood of Jesus!

Notes

Destiny

I command all obstacles to my destiny to be removed! I bind every hindering and devastating spirit that seeks to distract, destroy and derail my destiny, in the name of Jesus!

In the name of Jesus I terminate every journey into bondage and unfruitfulness designed for my soul and destiny by the enemy!

I will walk in the plans that you have for my life by your mercy and grace. You have ordained all of my days before one of them ever came into being according to Psalm 139.

I declare this will be a year of divine harvest for me, my family and my purpose! I call forth every area of my life to come into alignment with God's will for me. I will walk in the fullness of my calling and take possession of every promise you have secured for me through the blood of Jesus!

I am destined for greatness by the blood of Jesus. For your names sake, Lord, I will live as an example to show the glory of God in the earth.

Direction

Lord you order my footsteps according to your word. I trust you with every step that I take. I do not resist the moving of the Holy Spirit in my life. Lead me Lord as I completely surrender and commit my life to you.

I ask for your wisdom which you will give me liberally according to James 1:5. I will be led by your spirit. I shut off and resist every voice that contradicts your voice.

Forgive me Lord for doing my own thing, for rebelling against you and being stubborn. I thank you for never leaving or forsaking me. I turn from my way of life and the plans that I have for myself and turn to your way of life and the plans that you have for me, in the name of Jesus.

In order to follow you Lord, I forsake everything that you ask me to. I will not be led astray by wicked and deceitful spirits that are operating and influencing people and situations in order to ensnare me.

Notes

Disappointment

Why are you cast down, o my soul? And why are you disquieted within me? Hope in God: for I will yet praise Him, who is the health of my countenance, and my God. (Psalm 42:11) God, you restore me in every place that I have been hurt, offended, wounded or disappointed. I receive your joy and bind the spirit of heaviness in the name of Jesus.

I ask that you give me courage and strengthen my heart because I put my hope in you Lord! (Psalm 31:24)

Lord Jesus, use your spiritual eraser to wipe all painful and unprofitable memories from my mind. I will not dwell on those things that make me sad, hurt or disappointed. I have the mind of Christ and hold the thoughts and feelings of the Messiah.

I confess, repent and renounce the sin of unforgiveness and of allowing bad memories to poison my heart and my thoughts.

Lord, cleanse my mind of every sinful and destructive memory by the power of your blood.

I decree and declare the chapters in my life that are a mess are not my entire story! Hope in Christ will bring me to the promised future God has for me!

I decree and declare that when I go through disappointment; my spirit, soul and body are commanded to keep moving forward, in Jesus name.

By faith, I believe and receive that God has more ahead for me than anything that is behind me. He takes me from glory to glory and declares that the latter will be greater than the former.

Notes

_____
_____
_____
_____
_____
_____
_____
_____
_____
_____
_____
_____
_____
_____
_____
_____
_____
_____
_____
_____
_____
_____
_____
_____
_____
_____
_____
_____
_____
_____
_____
_____

Discernment

I have eyes of understanding and ears to hear the
voice of the Lord. The secret things of the Lord are
revealed to me by the Holy Spirit. He has given me
His mind and thoughts that I may walk in the wisdom
of God to know His ways. Thank you, Lord for the
spirit of discernment operating fully in my life.

Lord, give me the spirit of revelation and wisdom in
the knowledge of yourself.

I command the Lord to remove any spiritual cataracts
from my eyes!

Lord, open up my understanding and teach me the
deep and secret things of your counsel. Let me see
with eyes of the Spirit and walk in the ways you have
purposed for my life.

Lord, let every veil preventing me from having plain
spiritual vision be removed.

Lord, let the spirit of prophesy, revelation and
discernment fall upon the totality of my being. In the
name of Jesus divine revelations, spiritual visions,
dreams and information will not become a scarce
commodity in my life.

Discipline

Lord you have not given me a spirit of fear, but of love, power and a sound mind.

I ask for the fruit of self-control to manifest in my life at all times so that I can walk and live according to your will and your word, in the name of Jesus.

I crucify my flesh with Christ and bring it under subjection to the Holy Spirit.

Lord, in my weaknesses let your grace be sufficient to make me strong, in the name of Jesus.

Notes

Divine Alignment

I call every part of my being into divine alignment
with the will of God. Lord, whatever you're doing in
this season, don't do it without me!

Let every relationship and opportunity come into
alignment and compliance with the will of God for
my life. I surrender myself fully to you Lord and
bring myself under the subjection of the Holy Spirit.
Lead me in the path you have chosen for my life, in
the name of Jesus.

Father, in the name of Jesus, I completely surrender
myself to you as a living sacrifice. Anything that
does not align with your purpose for my life, I
command to be removed! Fill this temple with your
spirit and lead me to a lifestyle that is pleasing to
you.

Engaged to be Married

Father, I ask you in the name of Jesus Christ to send out your angels to all the corners of the earth on my behalf and let them bring to me the favor, provisions, blessings and materials needed for a successful marriage.

In the name of Jesus I bind, plunder and render to nothing, every spirit of marriage destruction.

Lord unite those that would bless me and keep all others away.

I renounce, break and loose myself from every ancestral marital curse or bondage, in Jesus' name!

Father, build a firm foundation in you with my fiancé. We choose to put you first from the beginning of our relationship. Prepare us for a life together that glorifies and magnifies you, in the name of Jesus.

Notes

Failure

In the name of Jesus, I refuse to be a candidate of selective misfortune!

By the blood of Jesus I break every spirit of failure assigned to my life! I am engineered by God to succeed! He has given me victory by the blood of Jesus, which causes me to triumph in all things.

Lord, send your axe of fire to the root of all problems that I have and cut them down in Jesus' name! Give me a divine prescription and solutions for every situation that I am facing.

I refuse to enter the valley of failure designed for me through generational curses and inheritance!

Let all stress of non-achievement, whether physical or spiritual, be uprooted in Jesus' name!

Notes

Faith

I am a believer and not a doubter. I hold fast to my
confession of faith. I decide to walk by faith and
practice faith. My faith comes by hearing and hearing
by the word of God. Jesus is the author and developer
of my faith. (Hebrews 11:6, 4:14, Romans 10:17,
Hebrews 12:2)

Lord, remove whatever is keeping me from being the
best for you.

In the name of Jesus I silence the prophet of doom
and failure targeted against my life!

I activate and release the gift of faith by the Holy
Spirit.

Every cloud of confusion that has enveloped my
mind must fade now, in the name of Jesus!

I cast down and bring to nothing every demonic
imagination against me and my faith, in the name of
Jesus.

I release faith to build by experiencing the reality of
your word working in my life. I ask that you, Lord,
increase my faith where there has been doubt,
unbelief and fear. Forgive me for not trusting and
relying on you for all things. I make a commitment
today to believe you and the fullness of your word.

Notes

False

Let every soulish prayer spoken against me, my family and my destiny, that was intended to disturb, and disorganize me, be blocked and overturned by the blood of Jesus!

In Jesus' name let the fire of God begin to cause destruction to any evil gathering or association affecting my life!

I break and overturn every spirit of slander, accusation and lies spoken by the enemy! I am covered by the blood of Jesus!

I silence and take authority over every voice that stands to condemn, judge and falsely accuse me! The blood of Jesus has cleansed me and made me free!

In the name of Jesus I silence every prophet of doom targeted against my life.

In the name of Jesus I command the spirit of confusion to come on all satanic prophets appointed against me!

I turn over to the hands of God every person falsely accusing me, spreading lies, slander, malice and gossip. Lord, for your name's sake, you will deal with all those that deliberately trouble me!

Notes

Family & Household

Father, in the name of Jesus, I thank you that you have poured your spirit upon my family from on high. Our wilderness has become a fruitful land. Justice, righteousness, peace and protection abide in our home in the name of Jesus!

I decree that my family dwells in peaceable existence, in safe dwellings and in quiet resting places! There is stability in my home, abundance of salvation, wisdom and knowledge!

For me and my household, we will serve the Lord. There will be respectful fear and worship of the Lord in my home.

I bind every spirit of strife and division over my family! I declare forgiveness and unity to flow in the name of Jesus!

All the needs of our family are supplied according to your riches in glory. (Philippians 4:19)

My family is securely built. It is founded on a rock, the revelation knowledge of your word and Jesus is the cornerstone of my home. He is Lord of my household. We submit our lives to your will and walk in your ways, in the name of Jesus.

Favor

Lord, forgive me of anything that stands between you and me. I repent of dishonoring you in any way, knowingly or unknowingly, and ask that the blood of Jesus cover and cleanse me.

I ask you, Lord, to open my spiritual eyes and ears that I may see my ways of error, pride, rebellion and disobedience that would prevent me from walking in your favor.

Favor begins with the fear of the Lord according to your word. I ask that my life would align with respect and admiration for you God. Bring course correction to every area that opens doors of disobedience in my life, in the name of Jesus. I submit myself to your Lordship and the will of God for my life.

Concerning my purpose in the earth, let the spirit of favor be opened upon everywhere I go.

I command to break into pieces every spiritual barrier and limitation to favor in my life, in the name of Jesus!

As I submit and surrender to the will of God and walk in the fear of the Lord, I command every area of my life in which I have lost favor, to be restored in Jesus' name!

I cover the favor of the Lord on my life with the blood of Jesus!

Fear

Thank you, Father for your love and protection. You said in Isaiah 41:13 that you will hold my right hand and to fear not, for you will help me! Thank you that you will never forsake me or fail to fulfill your word! I praise you for the working of your word; it is truth and life to me!

I command my flesh to not fear in any and all circumstances. I believe by faith that you are with me in all things. You will lead me by your spirit through the valley of shadow and death. I will not be overtaken but will overcome all things by the blood of Jesus! You told me to not be afraid of sudden fear, neither of the desolation of the wicked, when it comes. For you, Lord, will be my confidence and will keep my foot from being taken according to Proverbs 3:25-26.

You are my God and your love shall strengthen me. You will help me and you will uphold me with your mighty and powerful hand.

I decree and declare that my mind, body and spirit trust in you Lord and I make a choice not to be afraid.

You have loved me with an everlasting love. I decree and declare that your perfect love has cast out all fear within me. For fear has to do with punishment, and whoever fears has not been perfected in love. In the name of Jesus I bind any spirit of deception that would cause me to believe that I am not loved by you Father.

When I walk through the most challenging times of life, I will fear no evil, I believe by faith that you are with me and will continue to comfort me.

Let God arise and all my enemies be scattered, in the name of Jesus! Any that contend with me, the Lord contends with them, for you, Lord, are my protector.

I disband all the hosts camping against me and my home in Jesus' name! I will not be afraid for the terror by night, nor for the arrow that flieth by day' nor for the pestilence that walks in the darkness; nor for the destruction that wasteth at noonday: for the Lord will cover me with His feathers, and under His wings will I trust: His truth will be my shield and buckler. Every demonic networking against me is scattered and brought down in the name of Jesus! (Psalm 91:5, 4, 27:3)

The blood of Jesus is over me, my family and my ministry for divine protection. Every agreement with hell, death and the grave is broken in Jesus' name! I walk out my purpose with the boldness of God!

I arrest every demonic plan against me, my family and my purpose in Jesus' name!

I am preserved and protected by His blood! I will fear no evil for the Lord is with me!

Notes

_____
_____
_____
_____
_____
_____
_____
_____
_____

Forgiveness

Father, I come to you in the name of Jesus and ask that you forgive me of any and all offenses I have held onto or have caused. I cancel the effects of any seed of bitterness, resentment, anger and hurt in my life, by the blood of Jesus!

I ask you Lord to renew a right spirit in me and to cleanse my heart.

I confess my sins and ask for forgiveness Lord.

I release every person that has violated, trespassed or hurt me knowingly or unknowingly, in the name of Jesus. (Specify their name while praying this prayer.)

In the name of Jesus, I command every resistance to the moving of the power of God in my life, brought about by unforgiveness, to be melted away by the fire of the Holy Spirit!

By the blood of Jesus, I confess, repent and renounce the sin of unforgiveness, of allowing bad memories to poison my heart and my thoughts. I receive freedom and deliverance in Jesus' name.

You spirit of unforgiveness, loose your hold on my life in the name of Jesus! I command you to be separated from me! I place the blood of Jesus between you and me. I forbid you to ever return over that person and situation again in the name of Jesus! I am free!

Let the Lord place forgiveness in your heart by the Holy Spirit. I plead the blood of Jesus over you. I

85

pray that God picks up the pieces of brokenness and
fragmentation and restores your heart by His grace!

Notes

_____
_____
_____
_____
_____
_____
_____
_____
_____
_____
_____
_____
_____
_____
_____
_____
_____
_____
_____
_____
_____
_____
_____
_____
_____
_____
_____
_____

Fruitfulness

I decree and declare, I am blessed of God!

Let every design against my life that would bring destruction and failure, be completely nullified in the name of Jesus!

I break myself loose from the bondage of stagnancy and lack in the mighty name of Jesus!

Lord, destroy with your fire anything that causes your promise for my life to fail, no matter the origin.

Let every evil label fashioned by the enemy, against your promises for my life, fall off and be removed, in the name of Jesus.

Oh Lord, enlarge my territory and increase my borders for your glory.

I am created to be fruitful and multiply, to fill the earth and subdue it! I have dominion over the fish of the sea and over the birds of the heavens and over every living thing that moves on the earth. (Genesis 1:28)

Daily I shall increase in number, as my Father has looked upon me with favor and has made me fruitful to increase in numbers. I am in agreement with God's covenant with me! (Leviticus 26:9 NIV)

In Jesus name I nullify every curse of failure, barrenness and lack over myself. Let the fire of God strike down all demonic strongholds against me!

In the name of Jesus every curse of poverty, barrenness, unproductiveness and ineffectiveness is broken off of me! I am fruitful and plenteous! The blessing of the Lord overtakes me!

I decree and declare that all weapons of lies, false accusations, misrepresentations, slander, rumors and all satanic roadblocks are terminated in Jesus' name! Anything that is a hindrance to the blessings God has for me is arrested and overturned by the blood of Jesus right now!

Every spirit of fear, intimidation and manipulation against my success is bound in Jesus' name! Let all rough places be made plain in my purpose, dream and destiny! (Isaiah 40:4)

I deploy the hand of the Lord to go before me and make a way for impossible situations! His angels encamp around me and are well able to protect me! I engage the hosts of heaven to work on my behalf in the name of Jesus. (Psalm 27:3)

Every weapon the enemy forms against me is overturned in Jesus' name! Every evil tongue and negative word against my success is now condemned!

Let all strange fire (fire not from God) spoken against my life and purpose be quenched in the name of Jesus! I am protected and preserved by His blood to walk in the abundance Christ died to give me!

I pray an unleashing of supernatural favor, goodness and glory to flood my life, destiny, dream and purpose! I walk in dominion by the blood of Jesus! I will rule and have influence in the midst of my enemies!

In the name of Jesus I stand against all forms of darkened understanding, blindness and anything that would try to harden my heart from obeying heavenly instructions that would position me for blessings and abundance!

Let every snare of the enemy against me and my success be overturned by the blood of Jesus! I declare victory over difficult situations! Stubborn problems are being resolved by the wisdom of God!

Notes

_____

_____

_____

_____

_____

_____

_____

_____

_____

_____

_____

_____

_____

_____

_____

_____

_____

_____

_____

_____

_____

_____

_____

_____

Generational Curses & Blessings

Father, I come to you in the name of Jesus, I ask you to forgive me for all my sins and the sins of my forefathers. Let all transgressions and iniquities be cleansed by the blood of Jesus.

In the name of Jesus, I break every generational curse which may be in my family up to twenty generations back, from my mother's side and from my father's side.

In the name of Jesus I break and renounce every conscious and unconscious evil association with lodges, religious systems, idolatry, cults, the occult, witchcraft, wickedness and evil associations!

I declare the blessing of the Lord to overtake me and my family. We will serve the Lord and my descendants will walk in generational blessings, in the name of Jesus!

Let any prison door hindering my blessing open to me of their own accord after the order of the Apostle Peter.

As we hearken to the word of the Lord, blessings will rest upon my household (generations).

My children and children's children are richly blessed, walking in the obedience, goodness and favor of the Lord.

Notes

Healing

Thank you, Lord for your redemption. You were wounded for my transgressions, bruised for my iniquities and the chastisement of your peace is upon me, for by your stripes I am healed, in the name of Jesus!

Apply the blood of Jesus to every part of your body and ask for the presence of the Holy Spirit.

I loose and release myself from the curse of infirmity, in the name of Jesus!

I denounce and renounce any covenant of sickness formed consciously or unconsciously, whether by me or on my behalf, in the name of Jesus!

In the name of Jesus I command the convental spirits of the curse and evil covenants to go!

In the name of Jesus I release myself from every inherited sickness!

In the name of Jesus I command all hidden sickness to depart from my life!

Holy Ghost fire, burn up and flush out every satanic deposit in every part of my body!

Let every evil device against my health be overturned by the blood of Jesus! I overthrow the strongholds of sickness, disease, barrenness and weakness in my body! I am the temple of God and will walk in divine health in the name of Jesus!

93

I am redeemed from the curse of the law because
Jesus bore my physical and spiritual diseases in His
body.

In the name of Jesus I command the curse of sickness
to go!

In the name of Jesus the spirit of infirmity must
depart from my life!

Lord, wash me in your blood from the top of my
head to the soles of my feet, every fiber of my being
is cleansed, purged and purified in the name of Jesus!

In the name of Jesus I command my body to shake
off every arrow and spirit of infirmity!

Lord, you bore stripes and were wounded that I may
be healed and restored in my body. By the blood of
Jesus I receive the manifestation of my healing and
restoration of my health!

Notes

Healing for Patrick! 4-29-17

_____

_____

_____

_____

_____

_____

_____

_____

_____

_____

_____

_____

Hearing from God

I decree and declare the heavens open and the glory of God to fall on me now, in Jesus' name!

In the name of Jesus I command that my eyes and ears are open to receive all that God has for me!

In the name of Jesus, Lord, I ask that you would reveal to me anything that would block me from hearing your voice with clarity.

In Jesus' name I break every spirit of deception and bewitchment that would stop me from hearing the voice of God clearly.

Notes

Love

I will love the Lord God with all my heart, soul and mind and love my neighbor likewise. I choose to love maturely by the spirit of God.

Holy Spirit shed the love of God abroad in my heart.

Lord, give me an aggressive love that goes the extra mile to reach those who have been hurt and have put a wall of protection around themselves. In the name of Jesus let your love break through every barrier by my actions.

In the name of Jesus, Lord, I release and forgive every person who has wounded or offended me. Let me love with your love and possess your heart for humanity.

In the name of Jesus, Lord, give me your heart through your eyes and by your grace, that I may love those you have connected me with.

Negative Emotions

Father, I come to you in the name of Jesus, with every feeling of shame, hurt, bitterness, anger, depression and guilt. I confess my transgressions to you and receive your forgiveness by the blood of Jesus. You are faithful and just to forgive me and cleanse me of all unrighteousness.

Lord, you are my hiding place and you preserve me from trouble. You surround me with songs and shouts of deliverance. Heal me from everything that would keep me in a wounded place. You are my balm of Gilead. You bind the broken-hearted. I receive your healing for my soul, in the name of Jesus.

Jesus, I choose to forgive all those who have wronged me in any way. You will not leave me without support as I complete the forgiveness process. You are my helper; I will not be seized with alarm. What can man do to me? I will trust you, Lord, as the giver and source of life.

Notes

Peace

I break every spirit of confusion and strife in the name of Jesus!

Your word, Lord, declares that the peace of God which passes all understanding will keep my heart and mind through Christ Jesus.

2 Thessalonians 3:16 states, "Now the Lord of peace Himself give you peace always by all means."

I overturn and arrest every spiritual harassment that was sent to disorganize and confuse me in the name of Jesus! I have the peace of God.

Poverty

In the name of Jesus I break every spirit of poverty
on my life.

In the name of Jesus no devourer will destroy the
fruit of my labor.

In the name of Jesus I break every curse of failure
and lack.

I repent for any breaking of covenant with your tithe
and offerings, Lord. I ask and receive forgiveness for
disobedience the touching of anything that is holy
and belongs to you.

In the name of Jesus let the rod of iron fall on any
strange money that has passed through my hands.

Notes

Prosperity

I am the head and not the tail. I am blessed coming in and blessed going out. The Lord causes me to prosper for His glory.

In the name of Jesus let men bless me everywhere I go.

In the name of Jesus I retrieve my blessings, prosperity and wealth from every evil attack.

Let the ministering spirits go forth and bring blessings, prosperity and abundance unto me, in the name of Jesus.

Father, open doors of opportunity and favor in my life to create prosperity, in the name of Jesus.

Regeneration

Jesus, you are Lord over my spirit, soul and body for the word of God tells me that at the name of Jesus, every knee shall bow and tongue shall confess. I confess you as my Lord and Savior. I am made a new creation in Christ Jesus. Old things have passed away and all things have become new.

Father, through your Son you have delivered me from the kingdom of darkness and translated me into the kingdom of light. In Jesus, I have redemption through His shed blood and also forgiveness of sins. Jesus has blotted out the handwriting of ordinances that was against me and contrary to me, by nailing it to the cross.

I have been redeemed from the curse of the law because of the precious blood of Jesus. My mind is being renewed daily, so that I may prove, what is the good, acceptable and perfect will of the Lord.

Notes

Relationships

Lord, you are my ultimate source of love, companionship and friendship. I ask for divine connections that have been ordained by you in the name of Jesus. I ask and receive, by faith, discernment for developing and nurturing healthy relationships. Your word says that two are better than one, because if one fails, there will be someone to lift that person up. Bring the right people into my life and strengthen my current connections by the blood of Jesus!

I renounce and break all evil curses and bewitchment put on my marriage and covenant relationships in the mighty name of Jesus! I shut the door to the enemy and overturn every demonic assignment to destroy my relationships by the blood of Jesus!

Father, you know the hearts of people. Remove every veil of deception from my eyes so that I may see what you see and will not be deceived by outward appearances or flattering tongues.

Thank you, Lord, for quality relationships that help me to build a stronger character and draw me closer to you. Give me courage and grace to let go of detrimental and destructive relationships.

Lord, help me to love at all times. You said that you shed the love of God in my heart by the Holy Spirit. I open my heart to freely receive and release your love in the name of Jesus.

I take authority over and bind the strongman attached to the relationships you have assigned for my life and purpose in the name of Jesus. By the blood of Jesus I break all marital and family curses placed on my life through any spirit of witchcraft or iniquity.

Father, heal the past wounds and hurts which have controlled my behavior and speech that has caused damage in my relationships. Teach me to speak the truth in love in my home, in my church, with my friends and in all my relationships in the name of Jesus.

In the name of Jesus I command all family idols and generational curses from both sides of my parents release me, my marital life, my children and my family!

In the name of Jesus I break and release myself from every anti-marriage curse.

Father, I ask you in the name of Jesus Christ to send out your angels to all the corners of the earth on my behalf and let them bring to me the favor, provisions, blessings, wisdom and materials needed for successful relationships.

In Jesus' name I command all evil touch and all evil arrows shot against my family and my relationships to be completely neutralized.

In the name of Jesus I disband the host camping against our home and challenge every association gathered against our family with the fire of God.

I declare the Lord will reveal to me every secret behind the problems in my relationships. I have the mind of Christ and hold His thoughts and feelings. My eyes of understanding have been opened, in the name of Jesus.

Lord, use me as your instrument to develop a healthy community that submits to you and lives in divine alignment with your will and purpose, in the name of Jesus.

Lord, I pray the relationships that you have ordained as part of my destiny that have been broken, wounded and hurt; be restored by the blood of Jesus! Let the chains of bondage and unforgivenes BREAK in Jesus' name!

In the name of Jesus I break every spirit of division, strife and contention in my relationships and covenant connections! I decree your peace and unity for me, my family, my home and every God ordained relationship you have for me.

Notes

Restoration

I am delivered from this present evil world. I am seated with Christ in heavenly places. I reside in the kingdom of God's dear Son. The law of the spirit of life in Christ Jesus has made me free from the law of sin and death. In the name of Jesus all that the enemy has stolen is restored to me seven fold.

In the name of Jesus let all the powers encamping against my goodness and breakthroughs become confused and be scattered. In the name of Jesus, I will recover all that has been lost.

In the name of Jesus let all the powers of my adversaries be rendered impotent that I may pursue and recover all for the glory of God.

In the name of Jesus I command every evil stronghold and powers housing my rights and goodness, to be violently overthrown! I will be restored to my original condition and position by the blood of Jesus.

In the name of Jesus I pursue, overtake and recover my properties from the hands of spiritual robbers!

Every fragmented place in my life, spiritually, physically and emotionally will be made whole in the name of Jesus!

I declare restoration for every stolen blessing in my life in Jesus' name! Your latter will be greater than my former!

Notes

Salvation

Father, it is written in your word that if I confess with
my mouth that Jesus is Lord and believe in my heart
that you have raised Him from the dead, I will be
saved. Therefore, Father, I confess that Jesus is my
Lord. I receive Jesus Christ as my Lord and Savior
and make Him Lord of my life right now. I renounce
my past life with Satan and close the door to any of
his devices.

I am a new creation in Christ Jesus. I have a new life
in Christ, old things have passed away.

I thank you for forgiving me of all sins by the blood
of Jesus. I am saved and justified by faith. Jesus
became sin that I might become the righteousness of
God.

I am now your child, God. I have been born again
and am made new in Christ Jesus. Holy Spirit, help
me to live the life that God has for me.

Self-Esteem

I break all self-rejection, shame and feelings of worthlessness by the blood of Jesus! Any strongholds that cause self-doubt and hatred must come down in the name of Jesus!

Any word that was spoken over me, or against me that contradicts what God has said concerning me, or my purpose, is made null, void and ineffective in the name of Jesus! I cancel the harvest and impact of negative words against me by the blood of Jesus!

Father, forgive me for speaking against myself and rejecting your truth concerning who I am in Christ.

I break the spirit of rejection, guilt and shame over my life by the blood of Jesus. Who the Son sets free is free indeed!

God has delivered me from the powers of darkness and has translated me into the kingdom of His precious Son. In Jesus, I have redemption through His shed blood and also forgiveness of sins. Jesus has blotted out the ordinances that were against me, which were contrary to me, and took them out of the way by nailing them to the cross. I have a new name and receive myself as the child of God that I am through the blood of Jesus!

God, I thank you for blessing me with all wisdom from heaven. I thank you for a purpose that was created before my person. I praise you for allowing your word to be made manifest within me, now I can see, and know who I am!

117

Notes

Soul Ties

I come to you Father, in the name of Jesus. I repent
of any door I opened knowingly or unknowingly to
give the enemy legal access to my life. I break every
ungodly soul-tie by the blood of Jesus! I renounce
every act of wickedness, sin and disobedience that
formed an alliance to bind me with anyone not of
you, Lord. Right now the blood of Jesus sets me free
and severs everything that has me tied up spiritually,
emotionally, physically and financially, in the name
of Jesus!

Notes

Spiritual Awakening

I pray that my spiritual life is released from the hands of the oppressors and I bind every spirit of luke warmness in Jesus' name!

Father, quicken my spirit and give me eyes of understanding that I may see what is the hope of the riches of glory of the inheritance of the saints and what they are for myself and my family.

Father, I ask you now, in the name of Jesus, to give me the fullness of the Holy Spirit with power and complete alertness. I yield myself to you and surrender everything so the fullness of your will shall be done in my life.

Anything that would prevent me from walking out the perfect will of God and seeing in completeness is overturned and arrested by the blood of Jesus! I am quickened in my spirit man to live totally for Christ Jesus!

I delight myself in you and your word, Lord. I commit my way unto you and you will bring the desires of my heart to pass. (Psalm 37:5)

In Jesus name I am alive to spiritual things and dead to carnal things.

I will not shrink back in fear, or draw back from you, Holy Spirit, for then you would have no delight or pleasure in me. I draw close to you and honor you, in Jesus name.

I ask that every scale be removed from my eyes that prevent me from seeing and walking in the truth of your word.

I am alive in Christ and can do all things through Him.

Notes

_____

_____

_____

_____

_____

_____

_____

_____

_____

_____

_____

_____

_____

_____

_____

_____

_____

_____

_____

_____

_____

_____

_____

_____

_____

_____

_____

Thoughts

I will walk in the light of the glory of God and that light will shine into every remote corner of my mind and will bring revelation, clarity and understanding to me concerning my circumstances and purpose. For it is written: "Arise (from the depression and prostration in which circumstances have kept you), rise to new life! Shine (be radiant with the glory of the Lord) for your light has come, and the glory of the Lord is risen upon you! (Isaiah 60:1 AMP)

In the name of Jesus Lord, you are renewing my mind and restoring my soul!

I will meditate on the word of God and whatever is good and edifying, I will think on these things.

I hold the thoughts and the feelings of the Messiah.

Lord, I thank you for not giving me a spirit of fear, but, of power and of love and of a sound mind.

Notes

Unbelief

I break every spirit of doubt and unbelief in the name of Jesus.

Lord, send divine intervention to any situation or circumstance that creates fear, doubt, and unbelief, in the name of Jesus. Give me the gift of faith to believe for the impossible.

Notes

Unity

In the name of Jesus I break any spirit of strife and division in my home, my family, my life and my ministry.

Father, according to your word, let me be one with my brothers and sisters in Christ, even as you and Jesus are one.

Whatever the enemy has come to scatter I ask that you, Lord, would give me an anointing to be a gatherer. Let me be in one mind and one heart with you and your will, in the name of Jesus.

Notes

Victory

I already have the victory through Christ Jesus according to your word. (1 Corinthians 15:57)

I am always triumphant in Christ Jesus.

I can do all things by my relationship of resting and trusting in the Lord Jesus Christ. He has secured my victory. Therefore, I praise you God and bless your name at all times knowing that all things will work together for the good of those who are the called.

Vision

Though the vision tarries I will wait on it in the name of Jesus. Delay does not mean denial. Lord, help me to be patient and stay the course as that which you have showed me is coming to pass.

I ask you, Lord, to open my eyes and give me your vision for my life. In Jesus name ignite a passion on the inside of me to run with the vision.

In the name of Jesus I bind any hindering spirit that would shackle the vision of God for my life, calling, purpose and ministry.

Lord, give me the ability to write the vision and to make it plain so that he that reads it can run with it in the name of Jesus.

Lord, give me a vision for your heart and passion. Show me what you care about and help me to come in divine agreement.

Witchcraft

By the blood of Jesus, I break the power of all evil
controlling spirits against me and challenge every
association gathering against my family. Let every
word of witchcraft, action, spell, charm and hex
against me be overturned by the blood of Jesus.

In the name of Jesus I renounce and break myself
loose from all evil curses, charms, jinxes, spells,
hexes, psychic powers, bewitchments, witchcraft or
sorcery which may have been put on me or my
family. I command all the spirits connected and
related to these to leave me now!

In the name of Jesus Christ, I now claim deliverance
from any and all unclean spirits that may be in me.
Once and for all I close the door in my life to all
occult practices and command all related spirits to
leave me now!

In the name of Jesus let every spirit of Balaam hired
to curse me fall after the order of Balaam.

Let all evil monitoring gadgets fashioned against me
be paralyzed and destroyed by the blood of Jesus.

Let every evil effect of strange touches and evil
exchanges be removed from my life in the name of
Jesus.

Let every secret and spirit operating in darkness
against my life be revealed in the name of Jesus.

In Jesus' name I arrest every spirit of witchcraft, manipulation and conspiracy working against me, my family and my purpose.

In Jesus' name every weapon of wickedness being fashioned against me will not function!

Let every altar of witchcraft, familiar spirits and false religion in this country, in my community and in my home, be broken and come down in the name of Jesus!

In the name of Jesus I retrieve my blood or any other material from my body from every evil altar.

Let the counsel of the devil and those operating through sorcery against me be frustrated in the name of Jesus!

In the name of Jesus I command every satanic reinforcement that is against me, to scatter.

In the name of Jesus I cancel all evil vows that are affecting me negatively.

In the name of Jesus every power that wants to destroy my life, that is rebellious to the will of God for me, I command to be destroyed!

Holy Spirit, reveal to me every spirit of witchcraft that is operating and functioning in my life.

In the name of Jesus I withdraw my pictures, images and inner-man from the altars and covers of any evil associations.

By the blood of Jesus I reject, revoke and renounce my membership of any of the following evil associations: Jezebel spirit, marine spirits, water spirits, mermaid spirits, familiar spirits, witches and wizards, spirits of the dead and all other occult societies.

Notes

_____

_____

_____

_____

_____

_____

_____

_____

_____

_____

_____

_____

_____

_____

_____

_____

_____

_____

_____

_____

_____

_____

_____

_____

_____

_____

_____

_____

_____

"I would like to thank all of my intercessors, who help carry the torch throughout the world. I would like to give special thanks to Minister Sharon Toldson, whose labor is fruitful and prayers are powerful."